10624963

MY FIRST BOOK OF RHYMES

Illustrated by
Rie Cramer
Rhymes by Helen
Jill Fletcher

RIE CRAMER

Birds

Sparrows are birds
Finches are birds
Birds
    Can
        Fly
            Away
Missy has broken
Her cup of milk
  How
    Can
      She
        Drink
          Today?

RIE CRAMER

Good evening

"Good evening, Aunt Betty"
"Good evening, Uncle John"
My mother has asked me to say
Will you bring, Big Boy
And Baby, too
And come to tea, today?"

RIE CRAMER

Little pig

Little pig, little pig
  In a pig sty
Little horse, little horse,
  Legs held high
Little cow, little cow
  In the clover
Content ~ all over

Little fish, little fish
  In a net
Little doll, little doll
  Somebody's pet
Little baby, little baby
  In a bed
Curly ~ head

To bed to bed

"To bed, to bed,"
said Sleepy-head

"To eat, to eat,"
said Greedy

"Where is the food?"
said Let-me-see

In Grandmother's cupboard
I've got the key

Now, clap your hands
And sing with me

Ducks

In a pond
I see a duck
    Quack~Quack

And I see
A mother duck
    Quack~Quack

And I see
A father duck
    Quack~Quack

And I see
A sister duck
    Quack~Quack

And I see
A brother duck
    Quack~ Quack

And I see
A baby duck
    What Luck".

The little puppets

Hop little puppets
Let me see you dance

Dance little puppets
From far-away France

Rock-a-bye little baby
See the poodle prance

Prance little poodle
From far-away France

Saw the log

Saw the log
Saw the log
Saw the log in two

I would like
A piece of bread
I could share with you

But mother's out
And father's out
And I cannot get the bread

So I will share
My playtime with
The little mouse
INSTEAD

School days

On school days
On school days
Mary stays in bed
"I feel so awful," Mary says
"I cannot move my head"

On Sundays
Her sickness goes
And Mary hops from bed
She dresses in her finest clothes
A bonnet on her head

   And
       Goes
          To
            Church

A funny little native boy
   Liked the sun a bit
So in the desert without a hat
   He held a leaf over his head

Smile

Put on your hat
And drink your milk
I hear the lake
Is smooth as silk

We'll go for a sail
For many a mile
If you change your frown
Into a

S
M
I
L
E

Rain

It's raining
It's pouring
The rooftops are wet
The streets and roads are muddy, and

Wet As They Can Get

Watch out, watch out
Dear sister
The streets and roads are wet
We slipped and fell now look at us

Wet As We Can Get

RIE CRAMER

A.B.C.

A B C
What do you know?
A black cat walking
In
The
Snow

A B C
Who did you greet?
A cat with boots
On
His
Feet

A B C
What did he say?
Dry my paws and
We
Can
Play

Go to the market

Go to the market
To buy a cow

Clap your hands
And leave right now

Give to the man
A piece of meat

Give to the child
A toffee treat

Give to the lady
Asleep in bed

A gentle pat
Upon Her Head

Ice Cream Hill

Here is the key
To Ice Cream Hill
Fill your bucket
If you will

Give some to the boy
That sits in the chair
Give some to the girl
With the pretty brown hair

Give some to the boy
With the golden curl
Give some to the little
Baby girl
And
Take Some
Yourself

RIE CRAMER

In far-away Holland

In far-away Holland there stands a house
   Stands a house ~ Stands a house
In far-away Holland there stands a house
   As big as big can be

And in that house there lives a man
   Lives a man ~ Lives a man
And in that house there lives a man
   As grand as grand can be

And then that man he took a wife
   Took a wife ~ Took a wife
And then that man he took a wife
   As pretty as pretty could be

And then that wife she took a child
Took a child ~ Took a child
And then that wife she took a child
As sweet as sweet could be

And then that child she took a nurse
Took a nurse ~ Took a nurse
And then that child she took a nurse
As good as good could be

And then that nurse she took a groom
Took a groom ~ Took a groom
And then that nurse she took a groom
As strong as strong could be

And then that groom he took a dog
Took a dog ~ Took a dog
And then that groom he took a dog
As friendly as friendly could be

And then that dog he took a cat
Took a cat ~ Took a cat
And then that dog he took a cat
As gentle as gentle could be

And then that cat just sat and sat
Sat and sat ~ Sat and sat
And then that cat just sat and sat
And watched the baby cry
And
Wondered Why

Hurry , hurry

Hurry , hurry
Fall in line
Hurry , hurry
There's no time
Hurry, hurry
Form a queue
You hold me
And I'll hold you
T
I
G
H
T

Little bird

Little bird, little bird
When I'm in my bed
You wake me with your cheery song
Overhead

Tweet
Tweet
Tweet

Little bird, little bird
Now this must be said
I would like to sleep some more
I'm a sleepy head

Sleep
Sleep
Sleep

Little Tower

Little tower
On the hill
Tell me, please
If you will

Is that a flute
Way up there
Hanging and dangling
In the air ?

If that's a flute
What note was spoken
To make you tumble down

All
    Broken ?

Stork, stork

Stork, stork
What do I see
Is that a sister
Or brother for me ?

Shall I run home
Before it cries
And prepare my mother
For the big surprise ?

The three wee bunnies

In a cabbage patch
Under the sun
Sat two wee bunnies
Playing a drum
Another wee bunny wanted to join them
With his flute and make a too
                                    too
                                        too

The drummer said no and
too too did cry while they played tom
                                        tom
                                            tom.

RIE CRAMER

The bull frogs

Seven bull frogs
In a lake
On the farm
Wrapped in shawls
To try to keep warm
    No
        Use
ONE started to shiver
TWO started to shake

THREE started to quiver
FOUR started to quake

FIVE started to wither
SIX started to choke
SEVEN called out
"Bull frogs, Let's croak"

    KWAA
        KWAA
            KWAA
                KWAA

RIE CRAMER

Guess who?

There once was a woman
Making a cake
But the cream wouldn't whip
And
    The
        Oven
            Wouldn't
                Bake

The bowl tipped over
And made an awful mess
But someone cleaned the kitchen floor
Who was it
        Can
           You
             Guess?

Growing flowers

Little girl, little girl
Kneeling in the sun
Picking my flowers
ONE BY ONE

When you pick flowers
You have the fun
But flowers in a garden
Are fun for
      EVERYONE

Sleep, baby, sleep
Sleep, baby, sleep
I will sing a song to you
About a baby sheep

Sleep, baby, sleep
Sheep give wool to keep
A tiny little baby warm
Sleep, baby, sleep

Sleep, baby, sleep
Sheep give milk so sweet
To fill a baby's tummy full
Sleep, baby, sleep

RIE CRAMER

Bell-ringer man

Ding, Dong, Bell
Bell-ringer, ring your bell
My master will not eat this egg
He'd rather have bacon instead
I'll fry him some bacon in a pan
If you eat his egg Bell-ringer man

Ding
        Dong
                Bell

Easter

Palm, Palm, Easter~time
Three little children
All in a line
Carrying their offerings
Way up high
While Easter eggs fall from the sky
Palm, Palm, Easter~time

In a city lives a Duke
With a son who's name is Luke

If you ask him where's your cat
he takes off his little hat

With his finger, with his thumb
He will point out where he's from

Then he takes you by the hand
to his little wonderland

Sailing

The other day I was sailing
By the light of the silvery moon
Sailing the sea, Laridee
In the bowl of
          A Wooden Spoon

I laughed and sang
And sang and laughed
Until my spoon boat
          Broke In Half SPLASH!

Little maid

Little maid, pretty maid
Sweeping the floor
What are you holding in your hand
Is it a penny

          Or
               is it more?

Little Dog

On a snowy day
A little dog was found
Frozen was his broken tail
And he made not a sound

Along came John - the -butcher
Who said, "This dog is crazy."
Along came Mistress Pamela
Who said. "This dog is lazy."

Along came Mistress Missy
Who said "That is not true."
Along came Jeff-the~handy man
Who knew just what to do

Jeff took his little tool box
With hammer, nail and screw
And nailed the broken tail in place
The dog was good as new

The dog got up
And looked around
And ran to the woods
With a leap and a bound

Johnny, my boy

Johnny, my boy, wanted a horse
Wanted a horse to ride, of course
He called for his cat to be his horse
And his cat became his horse, of course

Heigh ~ ho

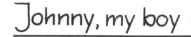

Johnny, my boy, wanted a park
A park to ride his horse, of course
He broke some eggshells to make a park
A park to ride his horse, of course

Heigh ~ ho

Johnny, my boy, wanted a whip
A whip to whip his horse, of course
He pulled a string to make a whip
A whip to whip his horse, of course

Heigh ~ ho

RIE CRAMER

Cockle ~ doodle ~ doo

Cockle ~ doodle ~ doo
I've got a game for you
Join your hands and form a ring
A child outside the ring must sing

Cockle ~ doodle ~ doo

Cockle ~ doodle ~ doo
I've got a game for your
Drop your hanky as you twirl
Behind some lucky boy or girl

Cockle ~ doodle ~ doo

RIE CRAMER

The Marionettes

We're rich marionettes
We're rich, rich, rich
Our shoes are new
Our clothes are fine
We sup on cake
And plenty of wine
We're rich marionettes
We're rich, rich, rich

We're poor marionettes
We're poor, poor, poor
Our clothes are rags
Our shoes have leaks
We haven't eaten
In weeks and weeks
We're poor marionettes
We're poor, poor, poor

RIE CRAMER

Skipper, Skipper

Skipper, Skipper
How is the tide?
I want to cross
To the other side

Lassie, Lassie
My pretty lass
The sea is as calm
As a sea of glass

Skipper, Skipper
What must I pay?
To cross the sea
This fine day

Missy, Missy
My pretty miss
You may pay me
With a kiss

Farmer, farmer

Farmer, farmer, what do you say?
Look at my chickens
Busy at play
How many eggs
Will they lay Today?

Farmer, farmer, what do you say?
Look at my rooster's
Feathers so gay
He is looking
His finest Today?

Miller, miller

Miller, miller
By the hour
Grind the wheat
To make the flour

Put the flour
In my sack
Mother said
To hurry back

She will bake
A special treat
That the children
Love to eat

Cakes and biscuits
Pancakes, too
Hurry, Miller
Hurry, do

RIE CRAMER

Where have you been?

Where have you been
In your pretty blue dress?

I've been to a party
At the home of Aunt Bess

What did you get there
Tell me, do?

Toffees and Toys
And something for you.

RIE CRAMER

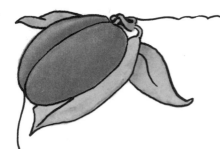

Mother, mother

Mother, mother
What shall I do?
Give me a job
I want to help you

Child, child
Milk the cow
It's very late
So do it now

Mother, mother
I hope I'm not bold
But I have no shoes
And my feet are cold

Child, child
Wear your socks
Or take daddy's boots
And cut off the tops

Angels

At evening when I'm sent upstairs
I get undressed and say my prayers
I pull the covers to my chin
And fourteen angels
    Tip
        Toe
            In

Angels stand around my bed
Angels hover overhead
Angels' voices do I hear
Whispering softly in my ear
    God
        Bless
            You
                Baby
                    Dear

Three little children

Three little children sat on a fence
One bright September day
And if you had been listening
You would have heard them say

I wish I was a teacher
To teach the A B C
I wish I was a nursemaid
With a baby on my knee

I wish I was a dancer
To dance before a crowd
I wish, I wish, I wish
The three children said out loud

To wish is to want
To want is to do
To do hard enough
Makes wishes come true